Policy Appra
and the Environment

A guide for government departments

LONDON: HMSO

ISBN 0 11 752487 5

COVER PHOTOGRAPH: 'Sunlight playing on beech leaf surfaces', *Martin Dohrn/Science Photo Library*

Recycled Paper

This document is printed on recycled paper comprising about 50% de-inked fibre and about 50% unbleached best white unprinted waste, depending on availability. Up to 15% virgin pulp from managed forests may have been used to strengthen the stock, depending on the quality of the recycled material.

The latex bonding used in the coating of the paper is fully recyclable.

LONDON: HMSO

Contents

Introduction

This guide for civil service administrators was promised in the Environment White Paper, *This Common Inheritance*. Many civil servants are involved in policies which have significant effects on the environment. The guide should increase awareness within government of the need to examine such impacts and offers a systematic approach to the treatment of environmental issues within policy analyses.

While the guide is written for those in central government who are charged with advising ministers on policies, it will also be useful in any public service where policies involve the allocation of resources. It may also be of interest to the private sector.

As a first step in the preparation of the guide, the Department of the Environment employed consultants to ask civil servants about their past experience and their current needs. Drafting then started on the basis of a range of views about the kind of guidance required. The final guide contains contributions from a variety of sources, mainly within government. Comments on the approach will be received with interest[1].

To White Hall, where met by Sir W Batten and Lord Brouncker, to attend the King and Duke of York at the Cabinet; but nobody had determined what to speak of, but only in general to ask for money. So I was forced immediately to prepare in my mind a method of discoursing.

The Diary of Samuel Pepys, 7th October 1666

---

[1] Comments on the guide should be addressed to EPE Division, Room A106, Department of the Environment, Romney House, 43 Marsham Street, London SW1P 3PY.

Chapter 1: Policy appraisal and the environment

1.1   A government's policies can affect the environment from street-corner to stratosphere. Yet environmental costs and benefits have not always been well integrated into government policy assessments, and sometimes they have been forgotten entirely. Proper consideration of these effects will improve the quality of policy-making.

1.2   This guide shows how environmental effects can be taken into account, both in environmental policies and in policies in other areas which have significant environmental impacts. This chapter looks at the need to integrate environmental concerns into policy appraisal and at the broad processes required. Subsequent chapters offer more detailed advice about ways of gathering environmental information and of using it in the development and appraisal of policy.

The process of policy appraisal

1.3   Ministers and the Cabinet make decisions about government policy on the basis of their judgements of the public interest. They base these judgements on advice about the policy options. Good policy decisions depend on their advisers having analysed the choices effectively.

1.4   The best way to do this is by a systematic appraisal of the policy options. Appraisal is the process of identifying, quantifying, weighing up, and reporting on the costs and benefits of the measures which are proposed to implement a policy. All the implications of the options must be analysed, including financial, social and environmental effects.

1.5   A systematic appraisal ensures that the objectives of a policy are clearly laid out, and the trade-offs between options are accurately identified and assessed. This gives ministers and the public the assurance that options have been fully thought out, and provides those who later interpret and build on the policy with a clear record showing how the decision was made.

1.6   The precise conduct of each appraisal will vary from case to case; depending on the complexity of the issues, the significance of the impacts, and the constraints, including the time and resources available. Policies tend to grow out of earlier decisions, so that clear starting and finishing points for an appraisal cannot always be identified. However, the key steps in systematically developing and appraising a policy are shown in Figure 1.1.

1.7   At the start of an appraisal the objectives of policy should be clearly specified and priorities assigned. In particular the ultimate objectives (those which the policy seeks to achieve) should be distinguished from the intermediate objectives (the means by which the ultimate objectives are to be achieved). This will allow the trade-offs between different classes of objective to be made explicit. Each

Figure 1.1:   *Steps in policy appraisal*

- **Summarise the policy issue**: seek expert advice to augment your own knowledge as necessary.

- **List the objectives**: give them priorities, and identify any conflicts and trade-offs between them.

- **Identify the constraints**: indicate how binding these are, and whether they might be expected to change over time or be negotiable.

- **Specify the options**: seek a wide range of options, including the do-nothing or do-minimum options; continue to look at new options as the policy develops.

- **Identify the costs and benefits**, including the environmental impacts; do not disregard likely costs or benefits simply because they are not easily quantifiable.

- **Weigh up the costs and benefits**, concentrating on those impacts which are material to the decision.

- **Test the sensitivity of the options** to possible changes in conditions, or to the use of different assumptions.

- **Suggest the preferred option**, if any, identifying the main factors affecting the choice.

- **Set up any monitoring necessary** so that the effects of the policy may be observed, and identify any further analysis needed at project level.

- **Evaluate the policy at a later stage**, and use the evaluation to inform future decision making.

objective should be revisited during the course of the appraisal in the light of the analysis of the options. A slight reshaping of the objectives may have a significant effect on the impacts and on the trade-offs.

1.8 General advice on appraisal can be found in other guides, notably in the Treasury's guide, *Economic Appraisal in Central Government*.[1] The present guide offers additional advice to ensure that environmental effects are fully considered during policy appraisal. This advice applies across the whole range of policies and programmes, and not just to those with direct environmental objectives.

Policies, programmes and projects

1.9 The distinction is often made between **policy**, the ways in which government seeks to achieve the objectives which it sets itself in a particular area, and **programmes** or **plans**, sets of related activities which give effect to policy. Programmes may in turn be composed of **projects**, discrete activities usually at specific locations.

1.10 Environmental impacts should be considered during the development of a policy, as well as at the level of programmes and projects. This is the only way to ensure that environmental concerns are integrated into the development of policy options. Furthermore, appraisal at policy level:

- permits proper appraisal of cumulative and global effects, since these cannot always be appraised fully at later stages;

- is essential in the case of policies which are not divisible into projects, such as taxation;

- allows ministers to anticipate and respond to problems which might otherwise become acute at the project level, and helps to gain public acceptance of the chosen policies.

1.11 Many impacts cannot be fully appraised at the policy level. Some environmental impacts depend upon choices made when the policy is put into effect by a programme or set of projects; for example, effects which depend on the locality of a project or on the choice of materials. In these cases the process of policy appraisal should be used to understand the broad nature of the impacts and to establish the framework within which environmental concerns can be addressed at later stages.

1.12 This guide is specifically addressed to decisions about policies and programmes, but much of its advice is also relevant to the

---

[1] There is a bibliography on pages 60–63

appraisal of projects. Indeed a number of the examples of specific techniques and approaches are drawn from project appraisals. Formal statutory procedures already ensure that the likely effects of major new development projects on the environment are fully understood and taken into account before those projects are allowed to proceed. These procedures include the provisions for planning control under the Town and Country Planning Acts and the requirement, under an EC Directive, for an environmental impact assessment (EIA) to be incorporated into the approval procedures for particular types of projects. The EIA procedures are an important part of the appraisal of projects raising environmental issues which this guidance cannot replace.

The nature of environmental impacts

1.13   This guide, like the Environment White Paper, adopts a broad definition of "the environment". The term is taken to include all media susceptible to pollution—air, water, soil. In these areas scientific analysis is the primary means of identifying cause and effect. The term also includes animal and plant life, and aspects of human experience, notably levels of noise and the impact of pollution on human health. The definition also includes environmental resources and assets for which judgements about environmental change are a more subjective matter, notably impacts on landscape, urban and rural conservation, and the built heritage. There is a checklist of environmental receptors in Figure 1.2.

1.14   Some policies and programmes are clearly environmental in that they have an objective which is directly concerned with the environment; for example, a policy to improve air quality by reducing emissions of particular atmospheric pollutants. But most areas of domestic policy have some environmental impact. These effects have not always been recognised.

1.15   Agriculture, industry, energy, and transport are obvious examples of policy areas with significant impacts. But others, such as communications, defence, planning and housing policies, can also have significant environmental implications. Many policies have environmental impacts outside the UK—including aid for overseas development and policies which affect shared resources such as the seas or the atmosphere. In general, any policy or programme which concerns changes in the use of land or resources, or which involves the production or use of materials or energy, will have some environmental impact.

1.16   Environmental impacts can, of course, be either beneficial or detrimental. New developments may have adverse effects on the

Figure 1.2: *Environmental Receptors*

Air and atmosphere	air quality; composition of the atmosphere; visibility.
Water resources	freshwater (surface and underground) for abstraction and consumption; sea water and marine resources.
Water bodies	size and situation of water bodies, eg lakes, rivers, reservoirs.
Soil	classification and/or quality; risk of erosion and landslides; water run-off; potential for contamination (waste disposal, etc).
Geology	rock types; mineral resources.
Landscape	characteristics and quality of rural and urban landscapes.
Climate	temperature; wind flow; rainfall and other climatic characteristics.
Energy	changes in light and other electro-magnetic radiation; noise and vibration.
Human beings	physical and mental health and well-being, which may include access to the amenity benefits of the environment.
The cultural heritage	urban and rural conservation areas; built heritage; historic and archaeological sites.
Other living organisms	birds, mammals, amphibians, reptiles, fish and invertebrates, aquatic and terrestrial vegetation.

The possibility of interactions between the above categories should be considered.

natural environment or may increase the production of harmful waste-streams. But there are, for example, major environmental benefits when derelict land is brought back into productive use. Equally, the Clean Air Acts, which were enacted principally because of concern about human health, had other beneficial effects, for example, on historic buildings previously damaged by smoke and sulphur dioxide.

1.17   With many policies which affect the environment, objectives can point in different directions. For example, new developments which harm the local environment may relieve pressures elsewhere. Policies may, therefore, lead to a mix of environmental improvements

5

and environmental damages. An important part of the process of policy appraisal consists of making such trade-offs explicit.

1.18   Environmental resources, unlike most other resources, such as manufactured goods or infrastructure, cannot always be replaced. The loss of a unique natural or cultural feature, ecosystem or species cannot be reversed. Even where the change is reversible the cost of rebuilding that resource may be substantial (for example, it will take many years to replace a beech wood). In some cases substitutes can be created for lost environmental resources, for example, it may be possible to create a new wetland in place of one lost to development. But such substitutes are rarely perfect. Policy analysis should always try to recognise irreversible effects, and ways of taking such effects into account within an appraisal are described in Chapters 3 and 4.

1.19   One implication is that where there is the risk of losing an environmental benefit for all time, the appraisal should be sure to recognise both present and future perceptions of environmental values. Rising expectations about environmental quality, coupled with a diminishing stock of relatively untouched environmental assets, may mean that the value to society of certain resources will increase over time. Therefore, even though the loss of an environmental amenity may not seem to be of major importance now, that same amenity may be more highly valued in the future.

1.20   It is not only future values of environmental assets which are uncertain. There may also be major uncertainty about the precise impacts of policy on the environment, both now and in the future. For this reason policy makers may wish to avoid the possibility of seriously adverse outcomes, and prefer to adopt a precautionary approach. This approach to uncertainty is described in paragraphs 3.13–3.17.

The public and the environment

1.21   In a systematic appraisal all costs and benefits need to be assessed, including environmental costs and benefits. People value both the direct use they may be able to make of environmental resources, and the very existence of these resources. Moreover, it is possible that the public might judge that environmental costs make a policy unacceptable, despite the economic or social benefits which it generates.

1.22   The public and the scientific perception of environmental value may differ. An impact which is of little public concern may be seen by scientists as a significant problem, and *vice versa*. In particular the views of the public about the relative importance of different risks to the environment are often not the same as those of the experts. The best way of ensuring that the public and the experts understand each other is to explain the scientific issues and to give people the opportunity to make their views known. Take full account of both scientific and public opinions, although in practice pressures of time and problems of confidentiality may restrict the amount of consultation that can be undertaken.

Summary: Chapter 1

- appraise policy options systematically, using the steps set out in Figure 1.1;

- explore all impacts, and do not limit the appraisal to financial or readily quantifiable impacts;

- be aware of all the potential environmental implications of your policy area, paying special attention to irreversible effects;

- in assessing environmental impacts, obtain technical and scientific advice, and pay heed to expressions of public concern.

Chapter 2: Gathering information on environmental impacts

Introduction

2.1   Whether you are dealing with a new policy issue, reviewing an existing policy or developing a programme for a policy already in place, set about identifying the environmental impacts at an early stage. Do not wait until the policy appraisal is nearing completion before starting to think about the environment. This chapter (with Appendix A) suggests ways of approaching the identification and, where necessary, the quantification of the environmental impacts of policy options. The next chapter outlines the actions which can be taken on the basis of an initial review of expected environmental impacts.

Identifying impacts

2.2   The first step is to list the potential impacts. The objects of this initial review, which is sometimes called scoping, are to show which areas, if any, need further analysis, and to decide what that analysis should be. There are a number of ways to start the process, for example, by looking at the impacts which have followed from previous activities in related areas, or by setting up a brief discussion with colleagues. Seek early assistance from your department's scientific or environmental advisers, or from the regulatory bodies. They may identify impacts which you had not recognised as significant. Public concerns may be gauged initially by the correspondence received, or by consulting voluntary organisations.

2.3   A number of approaches may be used to organise your thinking. Among the simple ones are the preparation of a checklist or setting out potential impacts in the form of a matrix. It is possible for anyone, not just a specialist, to make a first attempt to list the environmental impacts of a policy. This should be seen simply as an *aide memoire*, showing which areas need further work. It is not a substitute for seeking sound scientific advice from an early stage in an appraisal. Figure A.1 in Appendix A gives an example of the matrix approach: one axis of the matrix shows environmental receptors, such as air, water, soil; the other shows the activities associated with the policy, for example, land clearance, construction, use of water, production of wastes. The object is to identify those aspects of the environment which are likely to be affected by each component of policy. The use of a matrix is described further in Appendix A.

2.4 There is no foolproof way of ensuring that all the main environmental impacts have been identified. The essential points are:

- **Examine all stages of policy implementation**. For example, in considering an energy programme, look at impacts during the construction stage, the expected lifetime of plant, and the process of decommissioning.

- **Look at direct and indirect effects**. For example, the control of air pollution reduces emissions to the air, but the techniques chosen, like flue gas desulphurisation, may lead to an increase in discharges to rivers and sewers and to the generation of solid waste.

- **Look for wider effects**. For example, a house-building programme will mean more activity at quarries and along supply roads, as well as at the building sites; the reclamation of derelict land may appear to have substantially positive environmental consequences, but there may be the negative impact of loss of habitat.

- **Consult widely**. Colleagues in other divisions or in other relevant departments will bring a different perspective, and may spot potential environmental impacts which had not occurred to you.

2.5 When you have completed a preliminary list of the potential environmental impacts it should be possible to:

- suggest whether each impact is likely to be perceived as a gain (benefit) or a loss (cost);

- give some indication of the scale of impact, even though exact magnitudes may be unknown;

- start to recognise some of the trade-offs, in particular environmental gains bought at the expense of environmental losses elsewhere.

2.6 This information should be used to identify impacts which are significant and so are material to the choice of policy option. The significance of an environmental impact will depend not just on its magnitude or intensity, but also on the context. For example, where an impact is on a large scale, with national or even global effects, as with emissions from power stations, the environmental effects are clearly important. However an impact is also important if:

- it is of a complex or particularly severe nature, for example a policy which involves the release of toxic chemicals;

- it affects a site, or sites, of local, regional or national importance, such as a Site of Special Scientific Interest, or a National Park;

- its cumulative effect is likely to be severe, even though each single incident is not, for example the use of satellite dishes and the display of estate agents' boards.

There is no simple test of significance. But scientific advisers will be able to assist in making the necessary judgements.

Quantifying impacts   2.7   The next step is to predict more accurately those impacts which have been identified as significant at the policy level. This will probably involve some kind of quantification, though quantifying environmental impacts is not always straightforward. In some cases simple physical measures are available, for example tonnes of waste emitted. In others, while physical measures are available, scales have to be developed in order to estimate the impact on the environment. An example is that of noise, where the physical measure, decibels, has to be qualified in terms of duration, time of day, etc. There are other assets, such as landscapes, where physical measurements cannot be used to compare one case with another in purely objective terms. Finally, it may be possible to express environmental impacts in monetary terms (see Chapter 4), though this will often not always be possible at the initial stage of analysis.

2.8   Any form of quantification is likely to provide a better basis for decisions. Almost all appraisals will be built around estimates of quantities. Thus estimates of financial costs, both to government and the private sector, form a central plank of almost all policy appraisals. But an appraisal is also likely to contain forecasts of take-up, details of materials or equipment required, numbers of people employed, etc. Environmental impacts should be quantified alongside the other impacts of policy.

2.9   You will need the assistance of specialist advisers in your own or other departments to quantify the environmental effects. Some information will be readily available: scientific advisers should be able to assist you in using any data your department may hold, and can advise on external sources. Data on past impacts on the environment of related activities can be used as the basis for prediction:

Using existing data, we can predict within a range the amount of pollution that a power station burning a certain amount of coal each year is likely to emit.

We can estimate that a new village for 1,000 inhabitants will require a certain area of land to be cleared, and is likely to produce a certain volume of solid waste for disposal annually.

Where policy builds on previous decisions there may be a history of past projects to draw on, in which case you may be able to look at past environmental impact assessments (EIAs).

2.10   New research by your department or an outside agency may be required where the issues are complex or novel, or where information is scarce. Research can help to identify and quantify environmental impacts, to clarify complex interrelationships, and to explore policy options. The terms of reference of a research programme should be drawn so that it can, if necessary, be expanded later to include the study of new options, new environmental impacts and changing perceptions about environmental priorities. If you have commissioned external research, make sure the steering group includes representatives of all the appropriate scientific disciplines.[1]

2.11   Scientific uncertainties about impacts may be considerable. Ask advisers to indicate the full range of scientific hypotheses about a given impact and which scientists subscribe to which hypotheses. Even so, some of the most important environmental side-effects of previous policies have been quite unanticipated; examples are the health effects of putting lead in petrol, or the effect of CFCs on the ozone layer. The knowledge that your policy may have adverse effects which are currently unknown to science clearly does not make your present job any easier! Nevertheless, you should at least ask your scientific advisers to identify any current areas of disagreement, and identify any major differences of opinion in your report to ministers.

2.12   In quantifying effects, take account of the relationship between the physical results of the policy (for example, the output of a pollutant), and the associated impact on the environment. This is known as the **dose-response relationship**. Some activities may have results which are catastrophic for the environment, so that a relatively minor stress may produce a major impact. For example, an apparently minor pollution incident at sea could result in widespread destruction of aquatic life. More importantly, environmental damages may occur

---

[1] Further information on using research may be found in the Cabinet Office guide referred to in the bibliography.

only at certain critical levels. **Critical loads** are defined as the maximum loads of a potential pollutant which the environment can sustain before damage occurs. You should know whether it is possible for such effects to follow from the policies with which you are concerned. In these cases an objective of policy may be to keep pollution below critical levels.

2.13   Finally, some of the impacts identified may either be irreversible, or else very difficult to reverse (see paragraph 1.18). Make clear the conditions under which the impact becomes irreversible, and pay particular attention to such impacts in the later analysis.

Making uncertainty explicit

2.14   Predicting the precise impact of a policy on the environment is rarely straightforward. The information you have may be subject to significant uncertainty. There are several sources of uncertainty:

- **scientific uncertainties** about the basic relationships between the policy actions and the environmental consequences, possibly due to the long time scales over which many responses operate, or the complex interactions involved:

  > The link between burning coal and acid deposition is now generally accepted, but the link took time to establish, and there is still debate about the exact nature and size of the effects.

- **natural variability** of environmental phenomena:

  > For example, the quantity, timing and location of rainfall are key factors in assessing the extent of acid deposition.

- **lack of precision** in measuring environmental impacts:

  > It may be difficult to measure precisely the number of fish in a river, or to quantify the effects which policy has on the landscape.

- **uncertainty about the precise projects** or activities by which a policy will be put into effect:

  > In the initial appraisal of a programme of new house-building the exact sites involved may not be known.

2.15   Research may help to reduce uncertainty but will rarely eliminate it. You should consider whether the expected benefits from further research are likely to justify the cost. Where uncertainty does remain, you will need to know the range of possible effects, for example, high and low estimates of polluting discharges, or the probability that pollution control costs will exceed a given amount

This information will be used later to conduct sensitivity tests on the conclusions of your analysis. These tests are described in Figure 4.1.

Summary: Chapter 2
- start to assess environmental impacts at an early stage of policy development;

- perform a preliminary review of impacts so that you can decide which impacts need to be studied further: it often helps to draw up a matrix or checklist;

- look for impacts arising at each stage of policy implementation; include indirect and wider effects;

- use expert advice to identify and quantify the significant effects;

- indicate the degree of uncertainty, and the likely range within which effects may fall.

Chapter 3: Handling environmental information

Introduction

3.1   The central theme of this guide is the need to integrate environmental considerations with other concerns in the process of policy appraisal. Inevitably, resources are limited, and you will not be able to pursue every one of the leads established in your initial review. This chapter shows how the information you have gathered can be used to decide how, and at what stage, to respond to the various impacts.

3.2   Initial investigations may have identified any or all of the following:

- environmental impacts which are central to the policy decisions, or material to the choices being made;

- environmental impacts which are important but which cannot be taken into account until the project stage;

- significant environmental impacts which seem to be the concern of other policy makers who have already established the rules within which you must operate;

- impacts which are obviously so small that they will not be a major consideration during policy making and implementation;

- impacts which might be ameliorated, possibly at little or no cost to the overall policy.

3.3   Impacts will clearly be material if a decision cannot be made until the environmental dimension has been sorted out. Equally, some impacts are associated with the initial policy action so indirectly that it would be unreasonable to think of taking them into account in decision-making. Between the two lie various other impacts which to a greater or lesser degree can be associated with the initial policy, and which may be susceptible to changes in policy. In many ways these are the interesting, and the most difficult, cases.

3.4   Policy advisers are generally aware of the major environmental effects, though they are not always aware of the best way in which to take them into account in policy making. Equally, departments are no doubt rightly leaving out many minor effects from their appraisals—the question is whether they are ignoring too many.

A systematic review of impacts

3.5   Impacts should now be reviewed to identify the best means of dealing with them. Wherever possible, all impacts should be examined, not just those judged to require quantification. The review could follow from the categories listed in paragraph 3.2.

3.6   **All significant environmental impacts should be considered as part of a policy appraisal**. Some policies never give rise to an associated programme, and in these cases environmental impacts must be addressed at the policy stage. In other cases, the fact that there is a firm commitment to environmental appraisal of analysis at the project stage should not be taken to imply that environmental analysis is not needed at the policy stage. There are two reasons why the one does not preclude the other:

- environmental appraisals at the project stage are good at picking up local impacts, but those same projects may have national or even global impacts which can be addressed sensibly only at the stage of policy-making:

  the obvious example is the impact of any policy which affects energy use or transport on the emission of carbon dioxide, a greenhouse gas.

- the analysis of individual projects cannot take account of the cumulative effect of a number of possibly small projects, each of which may be individually fairly unimportant, but over time may have a significant or irreversible impact on the nation's stock of environmental capital:

  policies which affect land use can produce cumulative losses which will be greater than the sum of each of the individual losses.

3.7   **Some impacts may have to be taken into account at a later stage**. In many cases an analysis of environmental impacts is only feasible when the policy is embodied in choices about the location and type of particular projects. It is important that this need is fully recognised at the policy stage, and procedures set in place to conduct the necessary analysis during programme and project development.

3.8   **Some impacts are the concern of other policies**. Where policy proceeds within the constraints set by other regulators, for example, about emissions standards or the use of land, you need to ensure that your policy is keeping within the limits laid down.

15

Options which breach any limits or regulations will, of course, have to be reviewed.

3.9   Where it is clear that your policy will have to be framed within the context of broader rules and regulations, it is prudent to establish with the environmental regulators and other agencies concerned with the environment, that there is to be no new legislation or regulation which might cut across your policy. In some circumstances your plans could cause future problems for the environmental regulators.

3.10   **Some impacts may be put to one side because they are very small**. But be very careful before you decide that an environmental impact is immaterial to your policy. If there is any doubt about the exact nature of the effect it is better not to ignore it. Consult others who have an interest before making up your mind. If quantification does suggest that an impact need not be analysed at policy level—perhaps because it is not significant—review at project level may still be applicable.

3.11   **Many impacts can be ameliorated at policy level**. Efforts should, of course, be made to reduce major impacts. But in other cases minor, and possibly indirect, environmental impacts can also be reduced at little or no cost. At the project level there are certainly such cases. For example, moving the perimeter fence of a new airfield by 20 metres may reduce disturbance to a valuable natural habitat. Where decisions taken at the policy level have a direct bearing on subsequent use of resources, there may be analogous effects. Consider whether:

- greater energy efficiency could be encouraged, for example, in new buildings;

- low-waste technologies could be required in cases where production is central to the activities which follow from the policy, for example, in a procurement programme;

- recycling could sensibly be encouraged.

3.12   Where there is the prospect of an option favourable to the environment, recognise that there may be a case for preferring this option even if it is more expensive.

The precautionary approach

3.13   This guide suggests ways in which significant environmental impacts may be included in a policy appraisal. An approach which weighs up costs and benefits is appropriate in most cases, and this is the subject of the next chapter. But the uncertainty surrounding environmental impacts may require special treatment.

3.14   Research into environmental impacts may have revealed the possibility that there is a major threat to the environment. For example experts may believe that the introduction of a new chemical process could possibly produce highly adverse impacts. The problem is then to decide what action should be taken to respond to the threat. Further research may reduce the uncertainty. However, in many cases action will have to be taken before such research is finished.

3.15   Where there is no prospect of resolving such uncertainty in the immediate future, policy should be constructed around it. The Government's general approach to scientific uncertainty is that where there are significant chances of damage to the environment, it is prepared to take a **precautionary approach** even where the scientific knowledge is not conclusive, though the economic costs of the action must not be greater than is commensurate with the nature and degree of the risk involved.

> **For example, pesticides cannot be used until it can be shown that their use is not damaging to the environment.**

3.16   The precautionary approach has been adopted in areas with large scale impacts, such as climate change. A similar approach is sometimes suggested for smaller impacts. This relates to **regret** and **risk minimisation** approaches, where options are chosen to avoid the worst possible outcome. Since this approach would in some circumstances allow unlikely events to take precedence over policy options with large and certain benefits, it is important to do all you can to establish the likelihood that there will be an adverse effect.

3.17   If you expect the uncertainty to be resolved in the future, it may be advisable to start with **pilot projects**, which can be reviewed before a firm policy commitment is made. It is also possible to develop **contingency plans** which would set out the actions to be taken depending on the outcome of particular events. It is important to leave open as many future policy options as possible: cutting off potential alternatives may limit your, or your successors', ability to cope with future events.

Summary: Chapter 3
- identify environmental concerns which must be addressed at the policy stage;
- ensure that options comply with standards and other environmental commitments;
- identify impacts which should be addressed at a later stage, and establish the mechanism to undertake the appropriate review;

- consider whether impacts can be ameliorated at little cost;

- consider whether action must be taken to deal with impacts which pose significant threats to the environment, and in particular consider the possibility of a precautionary approach.

Chapter 4: The costs and benefits of policy options

Introduction

4.1   In all their decisions ministers need to weigh up costs and benefits. Ultimately their choices depend upon their political judgements, but these should be supported by as much detailed analysis as possible. The approach outlined in Chapter 3 can be used to identify the environmental impacts which need to be considered in the appraisal. This chapter outlines the means by which environmental impacts can be compared, both with each other and with other economic and social impacts.

Cost-effectiveness analysis

4.2   In some cases, policy may be constrained by existing environmental targets or objectives. These effectively predetermine the benefit side of the cost-benefit balance. Such constraints may come from previous political choices, domestic legislation, EC Directives, international agreements, public pressure or from some combination of sources. The first task should be to confirm that these constraints are real. It is tempting to accept constraints since they make decision-making easier, but they do not necessarily result in better decisions.

4.3   Where such constraints are real and binding **cost-effectiveness analysis** is the right approach. The objective is to select the option which achieves a target or goal at least cost. Cost-effectiveness analysis is generally the appropriate method to use to analyse environmental policies when a given environmental objective is to be achieved, or where the biggest difference between options relates to their costs.

> **An EC Directive limits the amount of nitrate in drinking water. This Directive is legally binding. In 1988 the DOE and MAFF studied the cost-effectiveness of two options to meet this directive: restrictions on agricultural practice, and treatment of the water before it is put into public supply.[1]**

[1] The references to the studies mentioned in this chapter are given in the bibliography.

However, while regulatory constraints are normally binding, they may be reviewed in the future, and ideally appraisals should consider the sensitivity of costs to small changes in the regulatory standard or the timing of compliance with the standard.

4.4 All costs should be properly considered, including the administrative cost to government, the compliance costs to business and any other economic costs. The guidance on the procedures for the completion of compliance cost assessments, referred to in the bibliography, should be followed. A policy can sometimes be made more cost-effective by substituting economic incentives for administrative controls. Annex A of the White Paper, *This Common Inheritance*, describes a number of applications.

4.5 Cost-effectiveness may also be the criterion against which other government policies are assessed. In this case you should try to supplement the analysis of the cost-effectiveness of each policy option with associated indicators of environmental performance. In some circumstances an option which appears less cost-effective may be chosen because it has a more benign net impact on the environment. For example, materials which pose less long term risk to the environment might be preferred as part of a procurement programme.

The framework of analysis

4.6 Where you are free to consider major trade-offs, a full "balance sheet" of costs and benefits should be the first stage of assessment. Within this framework you should aim to cover all costs and benefits, expressed both in quantitative and qualitative terms, to assess the uncertainty surrounding the results, and to show the distribution of costs and benefits between groups in the population.

4.7 Some costs and benefits can be readily valued in monetary terms, and in these cases the net benefits (benefits less costs) can be calculated. But other effects, including many environmental impacts, will, initially at least, be expressed either in descriptive terms or in quantities other than money. A clear exposition of costs and benefits, using a variety of means of description may be sufficient to make the trade-offs clear so that ministers have enough information on which to base a decision. For example, in some cases there will be strong evidence that either the costs or the benefits predominate.

4.8 But before accepting that such evidence is sufficient, make sure that the analysis is robust. If cost-effectiveness analysis is used, or if values of environmental impacts are not available, it is usually helpful to calculate the implied value to society of the suggested options. The choices you recommend will imply a value for environmental resources in terms either of the other benefits forgone to preserve the environment, or of the other benefits gained at the expense of the environment—is this implicit value acceptable?

> **An Australian report on a proposed nationwide scheme for compulsory deposits and refunds on beverage containers estimated that the net cost of the scheme to producers and consumers would be Aus$200–350 million. The analysis excluded the aesthetic benefits from any resulting reduction in litter. If the scheme were to be judged worthwhile it would imply that the public valued these benefits at least at this net cost. The authors concluded that this would be a very high value.**

4.9   The use of implicit values may not always give a consistent set of answers. Thus an examination of past decisions might yield a range of different implied values for similar environmental resources. An objective of the systematic appraisal of environmental costs and benefits is to remove any glaring disparities between the implicit values for apparently similar resources. However, since most decisions affect a bundle of environmental resources, the implicit cost of saving or losing a single resource cannot always be distinguished.

4.10   You should rarely be content with an analysis which is based on a single set of assumptions. **Sensitivity testing** to assess the effect of changes in assumptions on the policy choice is an essential part of any appraisal. In setting out the costs and benefits, and reporting on the analysis, you should show the degree of uncertainty surrounding the figures, and say how robust the analysis is to changes in underlying assumptions. It is then a matter of political judgement whether to take the chance of a bad outcome or to defer a decision until better information becomes available. Basic approaches to sensitivity testing are shown in Figure 4.1. More sophisticated approaches, which use the probability of different outcomes, are described from paragraph 4.31.

4.11   The **distribution** of costs and benefits is likely to be relevant to the political decision, and should be made clear in the analysis. Environmental costs are often borne by one group of people, while the benefits accrue to another, for example:

- **in some cases the construction of roads or power stations may impose a high local cost, in terms of environmental damage, on relatively small groups of people, while the benefits are shared among the population as a whole;**
- **increased use of energy now may cause problems for future generations through global climate change.**

Figure 4.1: *Sensitivity testing*

1.   The simplest way of testing for the effects of uncertainty is to think of "best case" and "worst case" (or "highest" and "lowest") scenarios for any impacts, costings or valuations that are part of the appraisal. The resulting range should then be included in the analysis.

> **For example under a business-as-usual scenario for emissions of greenhouse gases, the Inter-Governmental Panel on Climate Change estimate that the rate of increase of global mean temperature during the next century will be about 0.3°c per decade, with a range of 0.2°c to 0.5°c per decade.**

2.   Ideally you should always test the sensitivity of results to variations in assumptions using a range of possible values, rather than best/worst scenarios.

> **In an analysis of policy options relating to air pollution, sensitivity analysis might be carried out showing the effects on costs and benefits using a range of assumptions about:**
>
> - **emission control costs;**
>
> - **future emission levels (eg an assumption about growth in energy demand);**
>
> - **cause-effect relationships (eg the relationship between ozone and sulphur dioxide in causing crop damage);**
>
> - **the reduction in pollution achieved by a given policy measure.**

3.   As an alternative to varying single assumptions, you could test the performance of the policy given different scenarios, which might relate to different states of the world:

> **For example, UK air pollution policies could be analysed in the context of the following scenarios:**
>
> - **all European countries sign a new accord to reduce emissions;**
>
> - **50% of countries sign the accord;**
>
> - **business as usual.**

4.   A final alternative is to show how large a value would have to be placed on a given impact before a different decision would be taken. This value may be so big that, within a feasible range, whichever value were used, the same policy options would be chosen.

4.12   While the first stage in any analysis is to set out the information in a clear framework, it is often possible to augment lists of cost and benefits by further analyses which express disparate impacts in common terms. Where each option has a range of different effects, initially measured in different units, such analysis will make presentation of the choices more straightforward. This kind of analysis will also help you, and ministers, to understand the trade-offs better. More formal approaches are, however, all ways to draw out and make clear the implications of different decisions; none replace the political decisions which will ultimately be necessary.

Cost-benefit analysis   4.13   In **cost-benefit analysis** as many impacts as possible are expressed in terms of the monetary value which society places on them, and the net benefit is derived as the basis for policy choices. A discount rate is applied to costs and benefits which occur at different points in time. Discounting is discussed further in the annex to this chapter. There is an example of a cost-benefit analysis in Appendix B.

4.14   You will no doubt already have estimates of costs and benefits for parts of your appraisal. Estimates of the monetary implications of some of the effects may have been derived using information from relevant markets. You may also have estimates of the implicit costs of protecting the environment in terms of other benefits foregone, for example, if a factory were closed down to stop the pollution of a local environment. But it may be possible to go further and derive values for the public preference for environmental goods.

4.15   The use of money as a standard is sometimes a barrier to wider acceptance. Most people believe that there are some things which are "priceless" (in the sense that they cannot conceive of any sensible trade-offs involving these things). It may be considered immoral to place a value on goods such as clean air and water which are generally seen as a right for all. But a monetary standard is a convenient means of expressing the relative values which society places on different uses of resources. Valuation is, therefore, a means of measuring public preference, for example, for cleaner air or water, and is not a valuation of those resources in themselves.

4.16   One significant advantage is that most policy analyses use monetary or financial values for many effects, and valuation of environmental impacts puts them on a similar footing. In practice, many cost-benefit analyses include some effects which cannot be expressed in monetary terms, and there will always be important environmental assets which cannot be valued.

4.17 Careful consideration of valuation is especially important where an environmental impact is irreversible. In many cases the value of environmental resources can be expected to increase over time (see paragraph 4.1.4 in the annex to this chapter). The future value of an environmental resource may be substantial.

Ways to value environmental resources

4.18 If there is no market for an environmental good or service, there can be no market prices to use in a cost-benefit analysis. However in such a case there may be other ways to derive monetary values for people's preferences for environmental resources. Technical details of the main methods used are given in Appendix C. These methods are not always as difficult to apply as people think, though, as the following paragraphs indicate, all should be used with care. Doubts about some of the approaches suggested will only be resolved when there is a sufficient body of work which demonstrates the possibilities. This guide should be a spur to that further work within government.

4.19 Some techniques make straightforward use of market prices: for example, we have measures of the costs of the damage which pollution causes to marketed goods and resources such as crops or buildings. These are generally adequate measures of the value which people put on avoiding such damage.

A German study measured the damage which acid rain inflicts on buildings by looking at renewal and maintenance costs.

An alternative is to look at the cost of expenditures to avoid pollution damage (though it cannot be assumed that the value of the damage will necessarily be as great as this).

The cost of providing effective filtration in factories which pump waste into rivers might be used as a preliminary estimate of the value of avoiding pollution incidents.

4.20 Where an environmental resource may be lost, it is possible to look at the cost of providing its services by another means, or at the cost of creating an equivalent resource elsewhere.

The British Waterways Board has estimated the value of the drainage function of canals as the cost of providing alternative drainage (with the implicit assumption that if the canals did not fulfil this function the alternatives would be needed).

If the Cardiff Bay barrage goes ahead it will destroy mudflats used by wildfowl during the winter. The Development Corporation has undertaken to develop new feeding grounds at an estimated cost of £5 million.

However these methods do not measure public preferences. The value which the community places on the lost resource may be greater or less than this. Such figures should therefore only be used in circumstances where remedial action must be taken because of another constraint.

4.21   Wherever possible people's preferences should be assessed. An indirect way of measuring preferences is to use information about their activities in related markets to deduce something of the value placed on environmental costs and benefits. For example, prices in property markets can be used to measure the costs (like noise) and the benefits (like a good view) of different locations.

> **A study of rural house prices identified the impact of landscape attributes, such as proximity to woodland and water, on house prices.**

Expenditure on travel has been used to measure the extent of public enjoyment of recreational facilities.

> **A study has measured the leisure value of the canal network by examining the costs people were willing to incur to travel to canals.**

4.22   An alternative is to use surveys to ask people in a structured way what they would be willing to pay, or be prepared to accept by way of compensation, for a specified change in quantity or quality of an environmental good.

> **A study of the benefits of stopping the erosion of beaches used survey-based estimates of the values which people put on a day spent on different kinds of beaches.**

Survey-based measures can be used to put values on a wide range of environmental attributes. They are the only means of deriving values people place on the existence of environmental resources as well as their value in use.

4.23   Values derived from surveys depend to some extent on the context in which the questions are asked. For example, the values which people place on major policy options, like reducing the greenhouse effect, tend to be higher if the questionnaire is looking for a value for a single effect rather than for a set of values for various environmental resources. This is perfectly sensible behaviour by consumers, but it means that policy-makers must be aware of the context within which the valuation was made.

4.24   Exercises in valuation do not provide a single figure which is somehow the "right" number. Estimates of people's preferences are essentially measures of relative rather than absolute value. In many cases it will be difficult to arrive at anything other than a range for the plausible value of an environmental impact or resource.

For example, a study suggested that the value of the entire Forestry Commission estate to visitors lay between £14m and £45m.

Such ranges give a broad idea of the size of the other costs and benefits which would have to be set against a given impact on the environment. If you have no idea at all of the value on the environmental resource it is difficult to make any comparison.

4.25   In many circumstances valuation will remain impossible. But in these cases remember that the choices you recommend will still imply a value for environmental resources. Use these numbers to illuminate the choice.

4.26   Valuation techniques can be applied to good effect in policy making, but:

- there will always be some environmental effects which cannot be valued; you must guard against placing excessive emphasis on those effects which have been valued at the expense of those which have not;

- many techniques require specialist advice;

- whatever your success in deriving adequate values, there will always be a final need for political judgement about the weight to be given to environmental and other impacts.

Weighting and scoring

4.27   Where a range of objectives is to be achieved, different policy options will be better at meeting some objectives than others. Means must be devised for deciding how the options perform against the objectives as a whole. This may remain a matter of political judgement, or else a full cost-benefit analysis may be feasible. But another method is to score the success each option has in meeting the separate objectives, and then to bring all the scores together in a single weighted measure (hence the term **weighting and scoring**). Mathematical techniques can be used to weight the alternatives, but it is relatively easy for anyone to use the general principles to get a better feel for the choices.

4.28   In using this approach it is essential that the objectives are precisely defined. In particular, environmental objectives should be separately identified. The first step is to show how well each option meets the separate objectives. There is no need at this stage to express the effects in a common measure.

For example, various waste disposal options may be assessed against three criteria: cost, impact on local amenity, impact on global pollution. The policy options might be landfill, incineration, the production of refuse-derived fuel. The options are first separately assessed against each criterion. Suppose that Option A scores 100 on cost, but only 20 on the other two criteria; Option B scores 40 on cost, but 100 on the impact on local amenity, and 40 on the impact on the global environment; Option C scores 20:30:100.

There may then be no need to take the analysis further since useful information has already been obtained as the basis for decision. But there may be pressures to bring the figures together in single numbers, in which case weights must be applied to the performance scores:

To continue with the same example: if weights of 60:30:10 were applied to the criteria (ie 60 to cost; 30 to local amenity; 10 to global pollution), then Option A scores 68 and would be preferred (Option B scores 58, and Option C 31); if the weights were 30:40:20 then Option B would be preferred (it scores 60 against Option A's 42, and Option C's 38).

4.29   This sort of analysis will always be open to the criticism that the weights are arbitrary or biased. Sensitivity tests should be carried out on both the scores and the weights attached to the different criteria. Consider using weights based on a variety of sources, for example, a group of expert analysts, business or community groups, or opinion surveys. Each set of rankings is likely to show significantly different priorities. One possibility is then to test how different the decision would be if the decision was to be left to each of the different groups. This may help to determine those circumstances in which environmental considerations would become sufficiently important to offset the other concerns of policy. Final decisions about the appropriate weights to be given to different concerns must remain with ministers.

4.30   Weighting and scoring can be useful as a means of bringing out the various trade-offs, but it may be difficult to reach a consensus on the appropriate sets of weights. A major advantage is that effects can be expressed in qualitative, quantitative or monetary terms within the same analysis. Appendix B illustrates the use of weighting and scoring by Her Majesty's Inspectorate of Pollution (HMIP) in the evaluation of disposal options for low level nuclear waste. Further discussion of weighting and scoring can be found in the Treasury's guide to economic appraisal.

Analysing risk and uncertainty

4.31   Where the outcomes associated with different policy options are uncertain, the implications of this uncertainty may be assessed on the basis of qualitative judgements, drawing on expert advice and the results of similar decisions in the past. Experts should be asked to judge the likelihood of the different possibilities, using their experience and knowledge. Analysis could then use sensitivity tests, as described in Figure 4.1, to illustrate the range of possibilities.

4.32   But in other circumstances the nature of the risk may be such that a detailed quantitative **risk assessment** is required to identify the full range of costs and benefits and the likelihood that each will occur. This is work for experts and a comprehensive study would take several months. Even a quantitative analysis is unlikely to cover all eventualities, and qualitative judgements, again based on expert advice, will still be needed to come to the final decision.

4.33   The implications of a quantitative study of probabilities can be explored in detail by the use of **statistical simulation** techniques, now available on standard microcomputer programs. However a simpler, if less precise, way to incorporate probabilities directly into a cost-benefit analysis is to use **expected values.** An expected value is the average outcome which would be anticipated if the actions proposed were repeated many times. Such values are derived by multiplying the value of individual outcomes by the probability of their occurring.

> For example, under a policy option there is a 10% chance of the outcome being £10 million and a 90% chance of it being £1 million, so the expected value is £1.9 million.

4.34   In practice most policy choices will be single events, and the actual outcome will rarely equal the expected value. A further problem with the expected value approach is that it hides the full range of possibilities from the decision maker.

> For example, £1.9 million is also the expected value of another option where there is a 90% chance of a positive value of £10 million and a 10% chance of a negative value of £71 million.

4.35   It may therefore be more informative to use the information about probabilities to derive ranges or **confidence intervals** to show how reliable any estimates are. The larger the confidence interval the less confident you are of the outcome.

> For example, scientific research may conclude that the 95 per cent confidence interval for the biological oxygen demand (BOD) of domestic sewage is 320–380g/m³. This means that

only 5 times out of 100 would you expect the BOD to be outside of the range.

4.36   A risk assessment may be used as the basis for decisions about acceptable levels of risk. Comprehensive criteria for dealing with risk in this way have been established in the field of radiological protection:

- if a risk is too large it cannot be justified, irrespective of the associated benefits;

- if a risk is very small no further precautions need to be taken;

- where the risk falls between these levels, the issue is whether it has been reduced to the lowest levels practicable, bearing in mind the benefits flowing from its acceptance, and taking into account the costs of any further reductions.

In determining what is acceptable, formal methods, like cost–benefit analysis, need to be complemented by professional judgement and analysis of the lessons of past experience.

4.37   These criteria form the basis of the ALARP ("as low as reasonably practicable") approach which is applied in the regulation of industrial risks. The approach implies a bias in favour of reducing risk, provided that this does not impose an unreasonable cost on society.

Presenting the whole story

4.38   This chapter has sought to demonstrate that, within a general cost–benefit framework, there are several useful techniques which can be used to aggregate and compare disparate information, including environmental considerations. You may find it worthwhile to try out a number of different ways of analysing and presenting the choices. In particular, do not try to hide the details of the costs and benefits within a single overall total. Show the various components of the analysis in some detail and try to bring out the trade-offs. If you are to present the whole story no one technique can give all the answers.

Summary: Chapter 4

- analyse the impacts of the policy options within a broad cost-benefit framework;

- where possible try to obtain monetary values for environmental impacts; alternatively use weighting and scoring techniques to rank options;

- do not ignore those impacts for which no effective measures or values have been derived—describe these impacts qualitatively;

- conduct analyses to demonstrate the sensitivity of the results to different assumptions;

- give figures in ranges—most environmental effects and valuations will be imprecise;

- show the distribution of costs and benefits between different communities and groups;

- draw attention to the extent to which environmental effects are irreversible;

- bring out the trade-offs involved in each option; in particular, where no explicit valuations are available, calculate the values implied by the choices.

Annex: Discounting future costs and benefits

4.1.1   The object of discounting is to make it possible to add together costs and benefits which fall at different times. Discounting scales down the costs and benefits which occur in the future to reflect a preference for having extra income sooner rather than later, and for incurring costs later rather than sooner. The sum of discounted costs and benefits is called the **net present value** (NPV). If, in an appraisal, all costs and benefits could be valued, options with the highest net present values would generally be preferred.

4.1.2   For most applications within central government a rate of 6% a year in real terms is used for discounting costs and benefits which can be expressed in money terms. A real rate is applied to costs and benefits which are expressed in terms of a constant money value, rather than in terms of money values which increase with general inflation. For a full explanation of the use of discount rates, and details of exceptions to the 6% rule, reference should be made to the Treasury's guide to economic appraisal.

4.1.3   Environmental cost and benefits should be discounted, just like other costs and benefits. But environmental effects often persist far into the future. This means that discounting may be especially important: £100 million in 50 years time has an NPV of only £5.43 million when discounted at 6%. For this reason, it is sometimes argued that discounting discriminates unreasonably against policies which are designed to prevent long-term environmental hazards. The figure of 6% should normally be used as the standard assumption. But where exceptionally long-term policies are at issue, it may be appropriate to reconsider the assumptions made to derive the figure of 6% (this is a matter for discussion with your economic advisers).

4.1.4   The way to allow for the special features of environmental assets (or liabilities) is to pay proper attention to their future values. The value of most environmental resources can be expected to increase over time (though changes in taste may produce examples to the contrary). Rising values may result from the increasing scarcity of environmental resources or from increases in income, which mean that people are better able to enjoy the environment. The real costs of handling environmental hazards may also change in future; both increases and reductions are possible.

A US analysis of the Hells Canyon hydroelectric project showed that the recreational benefits of the scenic gorge would tend to increase over time, while the costs of the thermal power generation were likely to fall.

4.1.5 It is important, therefore, to ensure that before discounting takes place, costs and benefits are properly valued in terms of their future worth. For example, if the value of a resource is thought to be increasing by 2% per annum, then future values should be adjusted before the discount rate is applied. Such adjustments have to be approached case-by-case. In some cases it may be reasonable to assume that the value of an environmental asset will increase in direct proportion to national income, or perhaps in line with per capita income.

4.1.6 People may see it as particularly important to bequeath as good an environment to their descendants as the one they themselves inherited. This suggests to some that there is a case for altering the discount rate for environmental appraisals. But the correct procedure is again to make sure that the future worth of environmental resources is properly valued, and possibly to consider the use of a sustainability constraint (see paragraph C.9 of Annex C).

4.1.7 The bibliography gives references to other, more detailed, reviews of the use of discount rates in appraisals which involve environmental impacts.

Chapter 5: An overview of the appraisal process

Reporting and beyond

5.1   A systematic policy appraisal presents information in ways that make decision taking easier and provides a clear record showing how the decision was made. The purpose of this guide has been to show how the environmental impacts of policies can first be identified, and then analysed alongside other impacts within such an appraisal. This integration needs to be carried into the reporting stage and beyond.

5.2   When reporting the results of the appraisal to ministers, you may like to use the framework set out in Chapter 2 of the Treasury's guide to economic appraisal as a basis. However brief the report, where significant environmental impacts have been identified, they should be mentioned.

5.3   Action does not stop once the policy is decided, and your concern with environmental impacts should continue. Ensure that arrangements are in place to conduct the appropriate environmental assessments as projects are developed to put the policy in place.

5.4   You should also be sure that significant environmental impacts, particularly those which are uncertain, will be closely **monitored** as the policy develops, and that any contingency plans can be brought into operation should circumstances change sufficiently.

5.5   Finally, you should be clear how an **evaluation** of the outcome will be conducted later. It is important to check the extent to which the assumptions and forecasts in the appraisal have turned out to be valid in the event. This process can be used both to confirm the validity of the policy choices and to inform future decisions. Further information is given in the Treasury guide to policy evaluation, listed in the bibliography.

Reviewing the steps

5.6   This booklet has been designed to guide you through the development of policy. A checklist for policy appraisal is given in Figure 5.1.

Figure 5.1: *A checklist for policy appraisal*

- **Be clear about priorities, objectives and constraints**: list the aims of the policy and the constraints on the choices.

- **Consider the environment from the outset**: the earlier the environment is brought into the process of appraisal the easier it will be to integrate it into decision making.

- **Consider the key issues**: these include irreversibility, catastrophe, distributional effects, international issues, uncertainty and monetary valuation.

- **Identify a wide range of policy options** and continue to look at new options as the policy develops.

- **Seek expert advice**, consider the need for research to reduce uncertainty.

- **Identify impacts to be analysed or ameliorated at the policy stage**, and those which are better dealt with at project level.

- **Choose your method of analysis carefully**: use a broad cost-benefit approach, but try out different ways of analysing and presenting the choices.

- **Do as much as you can to analyse environmental effects**, even if time is limited you should always be able to identify the main environmental impacts.

- **Keep your appraisal under review**: environmental impacts may be more serious than was first thought, while new impacts may come to light during the appraisal process.

- **Monitor and evaluate the policy**; this will act as a check on the appraisal, and inform future decision making.

5.7 A simplified approach to the process is illustrated by Figure 5.2. There are many ways to conduct an appraisal, and the process tends to feed back on itself rather than proceed sequentially, as in the chart. Nevertheless, the chart does show the general questions which arise, and the types of actions you may take.

5.8 No single approach will supply all the answers. But the approaches which have been outlined should help to clarify the choices. The object should be to provide good information as the basis

Figure 5.2: *Appraising environmental impacts*

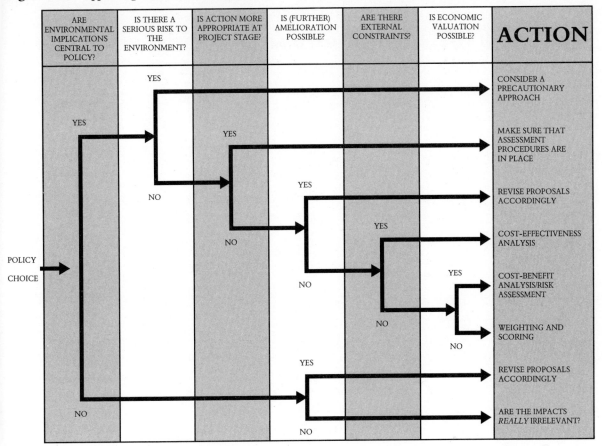

ARE ENVIRONMENTAL IMPLICATIONS CENTRAL TO POLICY?	IS THERE A SERIOUS RISK TO THE ENVIRONMENT?	IS ACTION MORE APPROPRIATE AT PROJECT STAGE?	IS (FURTHER) AMELIORATION POSSIBLE?	ARE THERE EXTERNAL CONSTRAINTS?	IS ECONOMIC VALUATION POSSIBLE?	ACTION
	YES					CONSIDER A PRECAUTIONARY APPROACH
YES		YES				MAKE SURE THAT ASSESSMENT PROCEDURES ARE IN PLACE
	NO		YES			REVISE PROPOSALS ACCORDINGLY
		NO		YES		COST-EFFECTIVENESS ANALYSIS
POLICY CHOICE			NO		YES	COST-BENEFIT ANALYSIS/RISK ASSESSMENT
				NO	NO	WEIGHTING AND SCORING
NO			YES			REVISE PROPOSALS ACCORDINGLY
			NO			ARE THE IMPACTS *REALLY* IRRELEVANT?

for ministers' judgements about what is best for society and for the environment.

5.9   The object of this guide has not been to tell you that it is easy to take the environment into account in policy appraisal. But it is necessary, and it is possible. Good analysis of environmental effects will enable you to improve—perhaps vitally—the substance, as well as the presentation, of a policy or programme.

5.10   The Environment White Paper committed the Government to a leading role in developing sensible and sound policies for the environment—it is up to all of us to meet the environmental challenge.

Appendix A: Using matrices to identify environmental impacts

Background

A.1   Matrices are a well–established tool for identifying and presenting information on environmental impacts. They have been used extensively in environmental impact assessment (EIA), where various authors have developed formal methodologies.[1]

A.2   The information which can be included in matrices ranges from short written descriptions, through the use of various symbols (ticks, crosses or more elaborate symbols), to numeric information which can be summed to indicate total environmental impacts.

A.3   The basis of all such matrices is that they relate the various actions to the associated impacts on the various environmental receptors (media such as air, water and land, living receptors and the built environment).

The use of matrices in policy appraisal

A.4   For the purposes of policy appraisal, a simpler and more flexible approach than that used in environmental impact assessment is appropriate. Matrices can provide an informal and simple approach in thinking about environmental impacts for non-specialists. Through their use, they draw out existing knowledge and raise awareness of environmental issues. However, in themselves they are not a substitute for seeking sound scientific advice from an early stage in the appraisal.

A.5   Matrices can provide a useful tool for thinking systematically about interactions between a policy and the environment and for identifying potential impacts. As a tool they are very flexible. They can be modified and refined as more information becomes available, and they can be prepared at different levels of detail, from an overall

---

[1] For example, in his book on EIA techniques, Leopold specifies 88 environmental characteristics and 100 project actions which should be included in a standard assessment matrix.

summary of impacts, to investigation of the particular pollutants produced by a given activity.

Preparing a matrix

A.6   It is useful to start with a matrix which looks in broad terms at the overall impacts of the policy on the environment. The actions resulting from a policy will then form one axis of the matrix. The other axis is formed by the components of the environment (receptors) which may be affected.

A.7   The first step is to identify the different actions which will result from the policy. This will be a basic step in any policy appraisal; it is not confined to environmental appraisal. In contrast to the use of environmental impact assessment at project level, there is no standard list of activities which can be used at policy level. Instead, you must think about the result which the policy is designed to achieve and the physical actions that will take place to achieve that result.

A.8   In identifying environmental impacts, however, it is particularly important to cover as many possible actions resulting from the policy as you can.

> **For example, a policy to encourage new villages would result in a construction programme. This would involve a number of steps, from preparing land, through the actual building process to occupation of the completed village. In practice, you would hope that existing natural features (such as trees) would be retained where possible.**

You should follow the policy through to its conclusion.

> **For example, in an energy policy which will result in the construction of new power plants their eventual decommissioning and subsequent site clearance should also be considered.**

A.9   There are no fixed rules determining what goes onto the axis of environmental receptors. The aim of the initial matrix is to be as comprehensive as possible in identifying the potential for environmental impacts. Therefore the categories selected should be as broad as possible to start with, covering the receiving environmental media (air, water, land), living receptors (people, animals, plants) and the built environment. The list of receptors should include receptors at any of the possible sites where a policy or programme could be implemented. At the initial stage it does not matter if some of the categories overlap, for example, that a pollutant released into the air will also affect human well-being and the growth of plants. A checklist of environmental characteristics is given in Figure 1.2 in Chapter 1.

A.10   The two axes form the framework of the matrix. The next step is to fill in the matrix cells, identifying where potential interactions may occur. The best approach to this step is often to hold a short "brainstorming" session, involving people with knowledge of the policy and awareness of environmental issues (not necessarily experts at this stage, although this may be helpful for particularly complex problems).

A.11   The aim is to mark the areas of potential impact in the matrix; it should also be possible to indicate whether the impact is positive or negative, and possibly to give a broad indication of the likely size of the impact. In the example in Figure A.1, B indicates a positive impact (benefit), C a negative impact (cost), two Bs or Cs indicate a sizeable impact. As well as "n/a" (not applicable) where there is no obvious impact, you may enter a question mark where you cannot yet

Figure A.1:   *Hypothetical impact matrix for new villages*

Policy components	Environmental components				
	Air	Water	Soil	Wildlife	Health/Amenity
Land clearing	?	C	C	CC	C
Access construction	?	C	C	C	B/C
Building construction	?	?	?	C	C
Water use	n/a	C	n/a	n/a	n/a
Sewerage	n/a	B/C	n/a	n/a	n/a
Transport access	C	n/a	n/a	C	CC
Waste production	C	C	C	?	C
. . . .					

Note: These markings are illustrative of the technique and not the result of a detailed appraisal.

determine whether an impact is likely. During the brainstorming session, you may also find that you need to modify or expand the axes of the matrix as you become aware of further actions which may result from the policy, or other aspects of the environment which may be affected.

A.12 The initial matrix will provide a useful tool, enabling you to make an initial identification of:

- the major areas of potential impacts;

- aspects of the policy, and/or the environment, where impacts are negligible;

- areas where more information is needed.

Preparing more detailed matrices

A.13 For the major areas of potential impacts, it may be useful to prepare a second, more detailed matrix to investigate impacts in more detail. In the new villages example we might focus on the effects of access construction on local amenity. The matrix in this case would list the actions involved in access construction on one axis (road building, intersections with existing roads, rail links, etc.) and the different aspects of amenity which would be affected (noise, dust, disruption, etc.) on the other.

A.14 The detailed matrices help to identify particular aspects of this issue which are likely to be important and will need further consideration.

Refining matrices

A.15 Matrices can be refined as further information becomes available, either through research or through further discussions with experts. Environmental experts within departments will be able to assist in ensuring that no environmental components have been omitted, and that all potential cause-effect links between the policy and the environment have been considered. Experts responsible for drawing up the policy should ensure that none of the actions arising from the policy have been omitted.

Appendix B: Case studies

B.1   COST-BENEFIT ANALYSIS:

Regulation of surface coal mines in the United States

B.1.1   The US Environmental Protection Agency (EPA) conducted a cost-benefit analysis of a proposal to list surface coal mines as a source category of air pollution. This would bring surface coal mines under the various rules that regulate the construction of new stationary sources of air pollution and modifications to existing sources. In particular, the action would limit particulate matter (PM) emissions of surface coal mines, and so would reduce PM concentrations beyond those achieved by existing regulations. At high concentrations PM can have adverse effects on human health.

Regulatory alternatives

B.1.2   Four regulatory alternatives were considered:

I   No further regulations beyond the existing ones.

II   New mines to be covered by the rules governing the construction of new sources; existing mines to be exempt.

III   New mines and existing mines built after January 1975 to be covered.

IV   Only those mines whose operations would have particularly serious effects on ambient air quality levels to be covered.

Environmental effects

B.1.3   Reducing ambient PM concentrations has been found to have beneficial effects both on human health and on the physical environment. Human health is improved by reductions in the incidence of cancer and of respiratory and cardiovascular diseases. Reduced PM concentrations also lead to less dirt being deposited on property, to less acidic deposition, and to an improvement in visibility.

B.1.4   To estimate the improvements in air quality due to regulation, the baseline PM concentrations associated with individual mines were estimated, and dispersion modelling was then performed to obtain the maximum off-site concentrations contributed by each mine. The difference between the baseline off-site concentrations and the concentrations which were predicted under the various levels of control was then estimated as the basis for the cost-benefit calculations.

Benefits

B.1.5 The categories of benefits analysed by EPA included morbidity, mortality, household soiling and materials damage, "visual range" and "plumeblight". Benefits were quantified by measuring peoples' willingness-to-pay for cleaner air. Ranges of benefits for new mines were estimated by making assumptions about the likely populations exposed. Benefits were measured in 1983 dollars using a 10 per cent discount rate.

Costs

B.1.6 Engineering costs associated with air quality improvement over and above the costs of current control programmes were calculated for individual mines. Emission control costs were estimated by looking at the current prices for new equipment. A surface mine production cost model was used to compute changes in the cost of production arising from forced reductions in output.

Cost-benefit analysis

B.1.7 The analysis compared the incremental costs and the incremental benefits of the four alternatives. The central results were:

Alternative	Net benefit (costs) $ million
I	(4.6)
II	(0.2)
III	(5.7)
IV	0.3

Alternative IV was, therefore, found to be the most economically efficient alternative.

Distributional analysis

B.1.8 All new mines were assumed to be located away from existing centres of population. The hypothetical population that was expected to be affected by PM emissions from mines included mine employees,

their families, employees of secondary businesses supporting th
mining activity and their families.

B.1.9   Economic impacts measured included changes in mark
prices and production, and the social costs of the alternatives. Th
EPA models assume that as the different levels of regulation impos
costs on new surface coal mines, market prices increase, surfac
production declines, and deep coal production increases in area
where the two technologies compete. Social costs represent th
increased costs of production due to price increases. The analys
suggests that regulation would primarily affect large mining oper
ations, and would not have much effect on the number of small
companies.

B.1.10   The results of the cost-benefit analysis were published by th
EPA as the basis for public consultation on the issue.

B.2   WEIGHTING AND SCORING:

**Assessment of Options
for Management of
Solid Radioactive
Waste**

B.2.1   The overall objective of this policy level study initiated by th
DOE was to "identify alternative strategies for storage and disposal o
low- and intermediate-level waste which would be the optimum from
a number of different viewpoints". A multi-attribute approach wa
used to determine the preferences between acceptable options for th
management and disposal of the waste. This approach was chose
because the subject is one on which there is a wide divergence o
opinion.

Analysis

B.2.2   The problem identified was the safe long term managemen
and disposal of seven different radioactive waste streams.

B.2.3   Five options were identified for the management of the waste
sea disposal, offshore boreholes, and three forms of land burial.

B.2.4   The impacts considered within the assessment included:

- costs (in £ millions);

- occupational collective doses of radioactivity (measured in man
  sieverts);

- collective dose to the public (in man-sieverts) nationally
  regionally and globally, from both storage and disposal.

Table B.1: Economic and Radiological Impacts of Different Management Options for Magnox Reactor Cladding Debris

Impact parameter	Management option						
	Sea disposal	Shallow burial	Engineered trench disposal (10yr storage)	Deep cavity disposal (15yr storage)	(45yr storage)	200yr storage then deep cavity disposal	Off-shore borehole disposal (15yr storage)
COST (£m 1985)							
storage cost	0	0	6.0	6.1	6.6	23.5	6.1
disposal cost	3.0	0.05–0.25	1.2	4.8	4.8	4.8	4.8
OCCUPATIONAL DOSE (man Sv)							
storage	0	0	0.08	0.09	0.14	0.43	0.09
disposal	0.06	0.02	0.14	0.15	0.08	0.02	0.006
SHORT-TERM EXPECTATION VALUE OF COLLECTIVE DOSE TO THE PUBLIC (man Sv)							
from storage	0	0	0.001	0.0015	0.0045	0.02	0.0015
LONG-TERM COLLECTIVE DOSE (man Sv)							
Local, regional and global							
up to 1000y	<0.01	0	0	0	0	0	0
1000y to 10,000y	0	0	0	0	0	0	0
beyond 10,000y	0	0	0	0	0	0	0
MAX INDIVIDUAL RISK IN A YEAR (y^{-1})							
Radionuclide migration	1.6×10^{-18}						
–inland site		0	0	0	0	0	0
–coastal site		0	0	0	0	0	0
Intrusion	6.2×10^{-17}	2.2×10^{-12}	2.2×10^{-12}	7.5×10^{-16}	7.5×10^{-16}	7.5×10^{-16}	7.5×10^{-16}

Source: Department of the Environment (1986), *Assessment of Best Practicable Environmental Options (BPEOs) for management of low- and intermediate- level solid radioactive waste*, HMSO.

Table B.1 shows a sample of the economic and radiological impacts of different options for dealing with one waste stream: debris from Magnox reactors.

B.2.5   To evaluate the acceptability of each of the options, four sets of weights were developed. These were designed to reflect distinct sets of views perceived to be held in society:

SET I   wishing to reduce costs, but taking into account the risk to workers in the industry, and short term collective doses to the public;

SET II   less concerned with costs; wishing to reduce risk to individuals and collective doses; low weight given to impacts in the future, both because of uncertainty and the small size of dose;

SET III very concerned with local impact, with high weight given to reducing risks from accidents at storage facilities; low weight given to cost;

SET IV the environmental option: low weight on cost, and a high weight on doses to the public, and on the future (due to fears of irreversible contamination, rather than simply health risk). The weight given to doses to workers is 100 times that for set I.

The weights are illustrated in Table B.2. They are not intended to illustrate any particular individual or group, but rather to make explicit the wide range of views which are held about the disposal of waste. In particular no attempt has been made to say which, if any, is closest to a majority view. Their purpose is purely to illustrate the issues to which people may attach importance.

B.2.6 These weights were then applied to the predicted impacts for each combination of disposal option and waste stream. Table B.3 shows the results when the four sets of weights are applied to the data

Table B.2: Illustrative sets of weights attributed to economic and radiological impacts for four sets of views perceived to be held in society

Impact parameter	Units	Weighting			
		I	II	III	IV
Cost	£m	10	1	0.1	0.01
Occupational collective doses	Man Sv	0.1	0.1	0.01	0.01
Public risk from storage (Expectation value of collective dose)	Man Sv	0.1	0.1	1	0.01
Maximum individual risk from disposal	Risk per year of 1 in a million	10	10	10	10
Collective dose to the local population from disposal	Man Sv				
up to 1000 years		0.01	0.01	0.1	0.1
1000 to 10,000 years		zero	0.001	0.01	1
beyond 10,000 years		zero	0.001	0.01	1
Multiplicative factor for collective doses to:					
regional population		1	1	0.1	10
global population		1	1	0.1	10

Note: Each impact parameter is multiplied by its weight to generate a value in equivalent units.

Table B.3 Magnox debris (from power stations): Weighted measures of economic and radiobiological impact

	Sea disposal	Shallow burial	Engineered trench	Deep cavity			Off-shore borehole
Storage period (years)	–	–	10	15	45	200	15
Weighting set							
I	30	0.5	70	100	120	300	100
II	3	0.05	7	10	10	10	10
III	0.3	0.005	0.7	1	1	3	1
IV	0.03	0.001	0.07	0.1	0.1	0.3	0.1

Source: Department of the Environment (1986), *Assessment of Best Practicable Environmental Options (BPEOs) for management of low- and intermediate-level solid radioactive waste*, HMSO.

in Table B.1. In this example, sea disposal of Magnox debris "scores" 30 for set I, while it scores only 0.03 for set IV. This reflects the fact that Set I gives cost a weighting 1,000 times greater than Set IV does.

B.2.7 Within any one group, the matrix also shows the relative preferences for different options. For example, within Set IV, sea disposal (weighted score, 0.03) is favoured over deep cavity storage for 200 years (score 0.3). This reflects both the cost of the latter option, and the relatively higher dosage to workers and the public.

Use of the results

B.2.8 The results were used at two levels. First, to identify the options which resulted in the lowest level of impact and, secondly, to illustrate the implications of choosing one option over the others for a particular waste stream, given the importance which society placed on the impacts.

Conclusions

B.2.9 Among the conclusions from the study it was shown that shallow or less deep land burial was the best option for low-level and short-lived waste; the increased costs of other options outweighed the small predicted differences in radiological impacts. This applied for all weighting sets. For Magnox wastes containing long-lived materials, 10 years storage followed by disposal in an engineered trench was the preferred option. For other waste streams, no best option was identified as the choice varied considerably depending on the weighting set being considered.

45

B.2.10   As the study points out, "the report is a decision-aiding, not a decision-making tool". It was also clear that it used the best information available at the time (1985), and that "all assessments will continue to be reviewed as better information becomes available from a continuing programme of research".

Appendix C: Monetary valuation techniques

C.1   This appendix outlines the available techniques for monetary valuation. Monetary valuation is about measuring preferences. It is not about measuring intrinsic values of the environment (that is, values which some people may argue reside in the environment itself, independently of any human perceptions). Economic values and intrinsic values are different. Values in things are not measurable, though they could be taken into account in decision-making.

C.2   In all cases the aim of economic valuation should be to elicit one or more of the following:

- preferences for an environmental improvement;

- preferences against an environmental deterioration;

- preferences for avoiding deterioration;

- preferences against foregoing improvement.

C.3   Figures can be derived either for the willingness to pay (WTP) for an improvement (or to avoid damage), or for the willingness to accept (WTA) compensation for environmental deterioration (or to forego environmental benefits). Studies show significant discrepancies that are still the subject of debate amongst the experts. Most notably, values derived by WTP studies are often substantially less than values obtained by WTA measures. Where possible attempts should be made to obtain both WTP and WTA measures, and to look for reasons for any divergence.

Some valuation terminology

C.4   Any environmental asset is capable of having several types of economic value. If a valuation exercise is to be carried out properly all components should be assessed:

Total economic value = User values + Non-user values

User values relate to the preferences people have for using the environmental asset in question—for example, the value of fishing in a river, of recreation at a beach site, of breathing clean air. **Non-user** values arise when an asset is valued by people who make no direct use of it. For example, many people care about the African elephant or an ecologically important wetland without ever having seen either. If an asset is valued because the person intends to see it some day, this is called an **option value**.[1] This may be seen as a kind of insurance payment to make sure the asset is still in existence at the time the individual decides he or she will exercise the choice of using it. Where such assets are valued, even though the person has not seen them in their natural state, and may plan never to see them, the value is called an **existence value**.

C.5   Total economic value will therefore comprise:

Total Economic Value = User values + Option values + Existence values

Option and existence values are likely to be potentially very important when the damage done or threat is to a unique or very well known environmental asset (the Grand Canyon, the Norfolk Broads, the Flow Country, endangered species etc). In such circumstances the non-user values should always be investigated. Only a survey approach can capture non-use values (see paragraph C.6.IV). This is why so much recent valuation work has used it.

Classifying valuation techniques

C.6   There are four broad categories of valuation technique that have been developed to a sophisticated level. The basic categories are summarised here. More detailed analyses of the individual techniques are contained in the figures at the end of this appendix.

I   Conventional market prices approaches
These approaches use market prices for environmental services. Some environmental changes show up in changes in the quantity or price of marketed inputs or outputs. In such cases the value of these changes in inputs or outputs measures the change in total welfare. If the changes are small, market values can be used directly. Where market prices are not an accurate guide to the relative scarcity of goods, for example due to monopoly power or the existence of subsidies, they may be adjusted to allow for the effect of these market imperfections. Such adjusted prices are often called shadow prices.

---

[1] It should be noted that some writers would regard option value as a user value rather than a non-user value.

Two market price approaches may be distinguished:

(i) The **dose–response** approach: for example, the welfare cost of a given level of pollution, which is associated with a change in output, may be taken to be the market value of that output. This could be used to value the loss of crop output from air pollution.

(ii) The **replacement cost** technique: takes the cost of replacing or restoring a damaged asset as a measure of the benefit of restoration. For example the cost of cleaning buildings dirtied by pollution. It needs to be used with some care (see paragraph C.7 below).

Other valuation approaches use market values but they are classified separately here (for example, the avertive behaviour approach, in section II(i) below).

II   Household production function approach (HPF)

In this approach expenditure on commodities which are substitutes or complements for an environmental characteristic are used to value changes in that characteristic. Thus, noise insulation is used by people as a substitute for a reduction in noise at source; travel is a complement to the recreational experience at the recreation site (it is necessary to travel to experience the recreational benefit). There are two distinct types of HPF approach:

(i) **Avertive Expenditures**, by which expenditures on the various substitutes for the environmental change are added together.

(ii) **Travel Cost Method**, by which expenditures on the travel needed to reach a recreational site can be interpreted as an estimate of the benefit arising from recreation at the site.

III   Hedonic price methods (HPM)

With HPM an attempt is made to estimate an implicit price for environmental attributes by looking at real markets in which those attributes are effectively traded. Thus, "clean air" and "peace and quiet" are effectively traded in the property market, since purchasers of houses and lands consider these environmental dimensions as characteristics of property. "Risk" is traded in the labour market: high risk jobs may well have wage "risk premia" to compensate for the risk. The two HPM markets of most interest are:

(i) **Hedonic house (land) prices**, which may be used for valuing characteristics such as air quality, noise, neighbourhood features such as parks, etc.

(ii) **Wage risk premia**, used for valuing changes in morbidity and mortality arising from environmental (and safety) hazards.

IV Experimental markets

These are survey approaches where a direct attempt is made to elicit preferences from people by questionnaires ("structured conversations"). Two kinds of questioning may take place:

(i) Eliciting values, where people are asked "what are you willing to pay for X or to prevent Y?" and/or "what are you willing to accept to forego A or to tolerate B?". This is the **contingent valuation method (CVM).**

(ii) Eliciting rankings, where the analyst is content to obtain a ranking of preferences. Values for goods which are not marketed, such as environmental goods, may then be derived by "anchoring" the preferences to the real price of something observed in the market. This is the **contingent ranking (CRM)** or **stated preference** method.

Some problems

C.7   In all valuation problems analysts should use careful judgement in applying techniques or using values. This is particularly the case with some commonly used procedures, which may be theoretically invalid as measures of preference, or which have major pitfalls in use. The major problem with these techniques is the extent to which they can legitimately be interpreted as measures of economic welfare.

C.8   The **replacement cost approach** seems to be a straightforward technique. If environmental damage is done, it is often possible to find out quite easily what the cost of restoring the damaged environment is. In some circumstances replacement costs may be used as a proxy measure of economic welfare costs. Using replacement costs to measure damage would be correct where it were possible to argue that the remedial work must take place because of some other constraint. Such situations will be quite widespread. For example, where there is a mandatory water quality standard the costs of achieving that standard are a proxy for the benefits of reaching that standard. This is because society can be construed as having sanctioned the cost (or at least the minimum cost) of setting the standard.

C.9   The replacement cost approach is also valid where there is an overall constraint not to let environmental quality decline (sometimes called a **sustainability constraint**). In these circumstances replacement costs might be allowable as a first approximation of benefits or damage. The so-called **shadow project** approach relies on such constraints. In this case it can be argued that the cost of any project designed to restore an environment, because of a sustainability constraint, is then a minimum valuation of the damage done.

C.10 However, in other circumstances, there are flaws in the use of replacement costs. If the remedial cost were a full measure of damage then the cost-benefit ratio (benefits divided by costs) of undertaking the remedial work would always be 1, because the remedial costs are being used to measure remedial benefits. To say that the remedial work must be done implies that benefits exceed costs, whatever the latter are. The costs are then a *minimum* measure of benefits. To pursue the water quality example, if the standard had clearly been set without thought for costs, using replacement costs as a measure of minimum benefits could be misleading. A standard based on BATNEEC (best available techniques not entailing excessive costs) tends to fit the replacement costs approach, but others may not. Careful judgement is required.

C.11 Another technique which can be misleading is the **opportunity cost approach**. In this case no direct attempt is made to value benefits. Instead, the benefits of the activity causing environmental deterioration—say, a housing development—are estimated in order to set a benchmark for what the environmental benefits would have to be for the development to be judged not worthwhile. Clearly, this is not a valuation technique but, properly handled, it can be a powerful approach to a form of judgmental valuation. It has been particularly useful in energy and mining developments.

Validity of valuation techniques

C.12 The validity of the various techniques may be assessed in the following terms:

- **theoretical validity**—is the technique consistent with the underlying economic theory of consumers' and producers' surplus?

- **convergent validity**—do the results of studies using each technique have the expected relationship with the results of studies using other techniques? For example, different theoretically valid techniques should give similar estimates of WTP. But we have no particular reason to say that any one technique is "correct". In the convergent validity test, then, we check to see if, say, HPM and CVM give similar results. If they do that should contribute to the credibility of the results.

- **repetitive validity**—does the same technique applied to similar contexts yield broadly similar values? This test is weak in that there is no *a priori* reason why the value of, say, a wetland in the

51

UK should be the same as one in Spain, even after correcting for income differences. Tastes may simply vary. Nonetheless, it does offer a little more information. The extent to which values in one place can be transferred to another place is, as yet, under-researched.

- **criterion validity**—does the technique yield results which bear a consistent relationship with real market behaviour?

Valuation techniques in detail

C.13 The figures on the following pages describe in greater detail the various techniques available. Guidance on further reading is given in the bibliography.

I	**MARKET PRICE APPROACHES**
(i)	**Dose–Response approach**
(ii)	**Replacement Cost approach**
Applicability	These approaches are extensively used where "dose-response" relationships between pollution and output or impact are known. Examples include crop and forest damage from air pollution, materials damage, health impacts of pollution. Since these approaches are limited to cases where there are markets, they cannot estimate non-use values. Replacement cost approaches are widely used because it is often relatively easy to find estimates of such costs. Replacement cost approaches should be confined to situations where the cost relates to achieving some agreed environmental standard, or where there is an overall constraint requiring that a certain level of environmental quality is achieved.
Procedure	**Dose-Response approach**: take the physical and ecological links between the pollution (dose) and the impact (response) and value the final impact at a market or shadow price. Most of the effort usually resides in establishing the dose-response links. Multiple regression techniques are often used for this.
	Replacement Cost approach: ascertain the environmental damage done and then estimate the cost of restoring the environment to its original state.
Validity	**Dose-Response**: theoretically, this is a sound approach. Any uncertainty resides mainly in the errors in the dose-response relationship: for example, where, if at all, are the threshold levels before damage occurs; are there discontinuities in the dose-damage relationship? An adequate pool of studies may not be available for cross-reference.
	Criterion validity is not relevant since the presence of "real" markets tends to be a test in itself—revealed preferences in the market place are being used as the appropriate measure of value.
	Replacement Cost: this is only valid in contexts where agreed standards must be met.
Expense	**Dose-Response**: this can be costly if large databases need to be manipulated in order to establish dose-response relationships. If dose-response functions already exist, the method can be quite inexpensive with low time demands.
	Replacement Cost: usually inexpensive as standard engineering data often exist.
Case Material	US Environmental Protection Agency (1985), *Costs and Benefits of Reducing Lead in Gasoline: Final Regulatory Impact Analysis*, EPA–230–05–85–006, Washington DC.

II	HOUSEHOLD PRODUCTION FUNCTION APPROACH

(i) **Avertive expenditures**

Applicability

This is limited to cases where households spend money to offset environmental hazards, though these can be important—for example, noise insulation expenditures; risk-reducing expenditures such as smoke-detectors, safety belts and water filters.

It has not been used to estimate non-use values, though it is arguable that payments to some wildlife societies can be interpreted as payments to increase the likelihood that conservation is successful.

Procedure

Although it is used comparatively rarely, this approach is potentially important. Expenditures undertaken by households which are designed to offset some environmental risk need to be identified. Examples of such expenditures might include noise abatement and reactions to radon gas exposure (for example, the purchase of monitoring equipment or visits to doctors). The technique needs to be managed by experts as significant econometric modelling is usually required.

Validity

This technique is theoretically correct. There are too few studies for it to be possible to comment on convergent validity. Because the technique uses actual expenditures criterion validity is generally met.

Expense

Econometric analysis on panel and survey data is usually needed, hence the method is fairly expensive.

Case Study

M Dickie, S Gerking and M Agee, "Health benefits of Persistent Micropollutant Control: the Case of Stratospheric Ozone Depletion and Skin damage Risks", in J B Opschoor and D W Pearce (eds) (1991), *Persistent Pollutants: Economics and Policy*, Kluwer, Dordrecht.

(ii) **Travel cost method**

Applicability The method is generally limited to the valuation of (mainly recreational) site characteristics and to the valuation of time. The latter is often known as discrete choice—for example, the implicit value of time can be estimated by observing how the choice between travel modes is made, or how the choice of good relates to travel time avoided (this has been used to value water collection time in developing countries).

It cannot be used to estimate non-use values.

Procedure A detailed sample survey is needed of travellers, together with their costs of travel to the site in question. Complications include the need to allow for the possible benefits of travelling, and the presence of competing recreation sites.

Validity Theoretically correct, but complicated where there are competing sites and multi-purpose trips. Convergent validity is generally good in US studies. Generally, the Travel Cost Method is very acceptable to official agencies and conservation groups.

Case Study K G Willis and J F Benson (1988), "Valuation of Wildlife: A Case Study on the Upper Teesdale Site of Special Scientific Interest and Comparison of Methods in Environmental Economics", in R K Turner (ed), *Sustainable Environmental Management: Principles and Practice*, Belhaven Press.

III   HEDONIC PRICE METHODS

(i)   House prices approach

Applicability

This is applicable only to environmental attributes which are likely to be capitalised into the price of housing and/or land. It is most relevant to noise and air pollution and to neighbourhood amenity.

It does not measure non-use value and is confined to cases where property owners are aware of environmental variables and act because of them (as with avertive behaviour).

Procedure

This approach generally involves the assembly of cross sectional data on house sales or house price estimates by estate agents, together with data on factors likely to influence these prices. Multiple regression techniques are then used to obtain the first estimate of an implicit price. Technically, a further stage of analysis is required since the multiple regression approach does not identify the demand curve directly. Often this stage of the analysis is omitted because of complexity.

Validity

Theoretically it is a sound approach, although the final estimate is not of a demand curve as such. Markets often may not behave as required by the approach. Data on prices and factors determining prices are often difficult to come by. The few tests of convergent validity reveal encouraging results.

Case Study

K G Willis and G D Garrod (1991), *The Hedonic Price Method and the Valuation of Countryside Characteristics*, ESRC Countryside Change Initiative Working Paper 14.

III	HEDONIC PRICE METHODS

(ii)   **Wage risk premia**

Applicability

This is limited to the valuation of morbidity and mortality risks in occupations. The resulting "values of life" have been widely used and applied elsewhere—for example, in the dose-response approach.

Procedure

As with the Hedonic Price Method, this approach uses multiple regression to relate wages/salaries to the factors which influence them. Included in the determining factors is a measure of the risk of accidents. The resulting wage premium can then be related to risk factors to derive a "value of a statistical life".

Validity

Theoretically sound, but labour markets often may not behave as required by the approach. Convergent validity may be tested against estimates derived from Contingent Valuation studies of risk reduction, but the wage-risk approach measures WTA not WTP.

Case Study

A Marin and G Psacharopoulos (1982), "The Reward for Risk in the Labor Market: Evidence from the United Kingdom and a Reconciliation with Other Studies", *Journal of Political Economy*, Vol.90.

| IV | EXPERIMENTAL MARKETS |

(i) **Contingent valuation**

Applicability

The contingent valuation method may be applied extensively since it can be used to derive values for almost any environmental change. This explains its attractiveness to "valuers". It is the only method which can be used to establish non-use values.

Procedure

The method involves setting up a carefully worded questionnaire which asks people, through structured questions, their willingness to pay, and/or accept compensation for changes in environmental resources. Various forms of bidding game can be devised involving yes/no answers to questions and statements about maximum WTP. While the raw data can give a preliminary idea of the nature of public preference, the survey results need econometric analysis to derive mean values of WTP bids. The literature tends to suggest that most sensible results come from cases where respondents are familiar with the environmental or other asset in question.

Validity

The literature has identified various forms of potential bias. *Strategic* bias arises if respondents make bids that do not reflect their "true" values. They may do this if they think there is a free-rider situation. But there is limited evidence of strategic bias. A *hypothetical* bias arises because respondents are not making real transactions. Expense usually limits the number of experiments involving real money (criterion validity), but some studies exist. Convergent validity is good. A further test of validity, construct validity, which relates the values derived to expectations about values of other measures, is the subject of much debate, especially the marked divergence in many studies between WTP and WTA.

Case Study

The case material is extensively reviewed in R Mitchell and R Carson (1989), *Using Surveys to Value Public Goods: the Contingent Valuation Method*, Resources for the Future, Washington DC.

IV	EXPERIMENTAL MARKETS

(ii)   **Contingent ranking**

Applicability

To date, the applicability of this procedure is not fully established, but it could be extensive. Only a few studies exist for environmental resources and these are confined to private goods—goods purchased in the market place. It is unclear how extensive the application could be for environmental goods but this is presently under investigation in the context of house location decisions.

Procedure

Individuals are asked to rank several alternatives rather than express a WTP. The alternatives offered tend to differ according to some risk characteristic and price. The idea could be extended to a ranking of house characteristics with some anchor, such as the house price, being used to convert rankings into figures of willingness to pay for those characteristics.

Validity

The validity of this method is not widely discussed in the literature but it appears theoretically valid. Too few studies have been conducted to test other validity measures. Initial results suggest that WTP from contingent ranking exceeds WTP from contingent valuation.

Case Study

W Margat, W Viscusi and J Huber (1987), "Paired Comparisons and Contingent Valuation Approaches to Morbidity Risk Valuation", *Journal of Environmental Economics and Management*, Vol.15.

Bibliography

General References:

A Allaby (1990), *Green facts*, Hamlyn.

S Pope, M Appleton and E-A Wheal (1991), *The Green Book*, Hodder & Stoughton.

S Simpson (1990), *The Times Guide to the Environment*, Times Books.

Further information on the environment may be obtained at the following libraries:

Department of the Environment library (071 276 4401 and 071 276 8361)

Environmental Unit at the British Library's Science Reference and Information Service (071 323 7955).

Imperial College Centre for Environmental Technology (071 589 5111).

Chapter 1: Policy appraisal and the environment

The Environment White Paper (1990), *This Common Inheritance—Britain's Environmental Strategy*, Cm 1200, HMSO.

Department of the Environment and the Welsh Office (1989), *Environmental Assessment: A guide to the procedures*, HMSO.

H M Treasury (1991), *Economic Appraisal in Central Government: A technical guide for Government Departments*, HMSO.

H M Treasury (1988), *Policy evaluation: a guide for managers*, HMSO.

David Pearce, Anil Markandya, Edward B Barbier (1989), *Blueprint for a Green Economy*, Earthscan Publications Ltd.

Chapter 2: Gathering information on environmental impacts

Norman Lee (1987), *Environmental Impact Assessment: a training guide*, Department of Town and Country Planning, University of Manchester (Occasional Paper No 18).

L B Leopold et al (1971), *A procedure for evaluating environmental impact*, Washington DC.

Department of Trade and Industry (1991), *Environmental Contacts: a Guide for Business*, DTI.

Cabinet Office (1989), *R & D Assessment, a Guide for Customers and Managers of Research and Development*, HMSO.

There are a number of published sources of data and information on the state of the environment. The following publications (most of which are produced annually) are likely to be of general interest and use:

Department of the Environment, *Digest of Environmental Statistics*, HMSO.

Welsh Office, *Environmental Digest for Wales*, HMSO.

Her Majesty's Inspectorate of Pollution, *Annual Report*, HMSO.

National Rivers Authority, *Annual Report*, NRA.

Organisation of Economic Cooperation and Development (1990), *State of the Environment Report*, OECD.

Chapter 3: Handling environmental information

Department of the Environment (1991), *Waste management paper No 28, Recycling*, HMSO.

Department of Transport (1983), *The Manual of Environmental Appraisal*, DTp.

Department of the Environment (1989), *Handbook of Estate Improvement: Part 1, Appraising options*, HMSO.

Department of the Environment (1991), *Environmental Action Guide, for Building and Purchasing Managers,* HMSO.

The *Energy Efficiency in Buildings* series, published by the Energy Efficiency Office, are useful guides to the techniques available in the construction and management of buildings.

Chaper 4: Costs and benefits of environmental impacts

Cost–effectiveness analysis:

Department of Trade and Industry (1990), *Guide to Compliance Cost Assessment*, DTI Deregulation Unit.

General texts on cost–benefit analysis include:

E Mishan (1988), *Cost-Benefit Analysis*, George Allen & Unwin.

R Sugden and A Williams (1978), *The Principles of Practical Cost-Benefit Analysis*, Oxford University Press.

D W Pearce and C A Nash (1981), *The Social Appraisal of Projects: a text in Cost-Benefit Analysis*, Macmillan.

Valuation techniques have been described in many journal articles and textbooks. The OECD is preparing a Manual of Environmental Appraisal which will include a section on valuation. That manual should be ready in 1992. The following are the best texts available at present:

J P Barde, D W Pearce (1991), *Valuing the Environment*, Earthscan.

A Kneese (1984), *Measuring the Benefits of Clean Air and Water*, Resources for the Future, Washington DC.

D W Pearce and A Markandya (1989), *Environmental Policy Benefits: Monetary Valuation*, OECD.

J Winpenny (1991), *Valuing the Environment: A Guide to Economic Appraisal*, HMSO.

A M Freeman (1979), *The Benefits of Environmental Improvement*, Johns Hopkins University Press, Baltimore.

R K Turner and I Bateman (1990), *A Critical Review of Monetary Assessment Methods and Techniques*, Environmental Appraisal Group, University of East Anglia.

N Hanley (1990), *Valuation of environmental effects*, ESU Research Paper No 22, Industry Department for Scotland/Scottish Development Agency.

P O Johansson (1987), *The Economic Theory and Measurement of Environmental Benefits*, Cambridge University Press.

J Braden and C Kolstead (1991), *Measuring the Demand for Environmental Quality*, North Holland—Elsevier, Amsterdam.

Weighting and scoring and related techniques are described in a number of books. The first reference below is an example of the technique in practice.

Department of the Environment (1986), *Assessment of Best Practicable Environmental Options (BPEOs) for management of low- and intermediate-level solid radioactive waste*, HMSO.

D E Bell et al (eds) (1977), *Conflicting objectives in decisions*, John Wiley & Sons.

R L Keeney, H Raiffa (1976), *Decisions with multiple objectives*, Wiley, New York.

Among the many references on risk and uncertainty are:

M Granger Morgan and Max Henrion (1990), *Uncertainty: a guide to dealing with uncertainty in quantitative risk and policy analysis*, Cambridge University Press.

A M Finkel (1990), *Confronting uncertainty in risk management, a guide for decision-makers*, Resources for the Future, Washington DC.

Health and Safety Executive (1988), *The Tolerability of Risk from Nuclear Power Stations,* HMSO.

Health and Safety Executive (1989), *Quantified risk assessment: its input to decision making*, HMSO.

The references to the valuation studies mentioned in Chapter 4 are:

Paragraph:	Reference:
Figure 4.1	Intergovernmental Panel on Climate Change (1990), *Climate Change, The IPCC Scientific Assessment,* Cambridge University Press.

4.3	Department of Environment and the Ministry of Agriculture, Fisheries and Food (1989), *The Nitrates Issue*, HMSO.
4.8	Industries Assistance Commission (1987), *Glass and Glassware*, Report No 404, Australian Government Publishing Service.
4.19	I Heinz (1986), *On economic evaluation of property damage due to air pollution, in costs of environmental pollution*, quoted in W & E Schulz (1990), *The use of benefit estimates in environmental decision-making: case study on Germany*, OECD.
4.21	K G Willis and G D Garrod (forthcoming), "Valuing goods' characteristics: an application of the hedonic price method to environmental attributes", *Journal of Environmental Management*.
4.21	K G Willis and G D Garrod (1990), *Valuing open access recreation on inland waterways*, ESRC Countryside Change Initiative Working Paper 12.
4.22	C Green, S Tunstall, E Penning-Rowsell, A Coker (1990), *The benefits of coast protection: results from testing the Contingent Valuation Method (CVM) for valuing beach recreation*, Flood Hazard Research Centre, Middlesex Polytechnic.
4.24	K G Willis and J F Benson (1989), "Recreational value of forests", *Forestry*, Volume 62, No 2, pp93–109.
Annex	A C Fisher (1981), *Resource and Environmental Economics*, Cambridge University Press.

Glossary

ALARP (or ALARA)	'As low as reasonably practicable', (or 'achievable'), a requirement in risk management.
AONB	'Area of outstanding natural beauty', an area of scenic beauty and scientific importance so designated by the Countryside Commission
APPRAISAL	The process of defining and examining options, and of weighting costs and benefits before a decision is made.
BATNEEC	'Best available techniques not entailing excessive cost.'
CATASTROPHE	An impact of major global or local importance; often irreversible.
CONSUMERS' AND PRODUCERS' SURPLUS	Concepts from economics which refer to the welfare received by economic agents.
CONTINGENT RANKING	A valuation technique that uses survey questions to elicit people's values by ordering their preferences. See Appendix C, IV (ii).
CONTINGENT VALUATION	A valuation technique that uses direct survey questions to the public. See Appendix C, IV (i).
COST-EFFECTIVENESS ANALYSIS	A method that finds the option that meets a predefined objective at minimum cost.
CRITICAL LOAD	The maximum level of a pollutant that can be tolerated by the environment without damage.

DISCOUNTING	The technique of applying a discount rate to convert future monetary amounts to their equivalent value in today's terms.
DOSE-RESPONSE RELATIONSHIP	The relationship between the level of a pollutant and the environmental impact.
ENVIRONMENTAL IMPACT ASSESSMENT (in the UK the term Environmental Assessment is used interchangably)	A technique for identifying the environmental effects of development projects and an important element in the procedure in land use planning for certain new developments. Procedures include the preparation of an environmental statement and appropriate public consultations prior to the granting of consent for the project.
ENVIRONMENTAL VALUE	A measure of the public's preferences for non-marketed environmental goods and services.
EVALUATION	The ex-post examination of the effects of a policy.
EXISTENCE VALUE	Values placed on environmental assets, flora or fauna, which are independent of their use by human beings, relating instead to people's satisfaction in knowing that the object exists.
HEDONIC PRICING	A technique which uses differences in market prices (for example, house prices) to establish environmental values. See Appendix C, III (i) and (ii)
IMPACT MATRIX	A multi-dimensional array used to show the effects of policy actions on the environment. See Appendix A.
IRREVERSIBLITY	When a potential outcome cannot be reversed, or possibly reversed only at unreasonable cost.
MULTI-ATTRIBUTE and MULTI-CRITERIA ANALYSIS	Particular versions of the 'weighing and scoring' (qv) approach to the analysis of policy options.
NET PRESENT VALUE	The sum of discounted future costs and benefits.

OPTION VALUE	An environmental value relating to the option to use an asset in the future.
PRECAUTIONARY APPROACH	A decision to take avoiding action based on the possibility of significant environmental damage, even before there is conclusive scientific evidence that the damage will occur.
RISK	The probability of an adverse outcome, or (sometimes) the likelihood attached to different outcomes.
RISK MINIMISATION	A criterion for policy choices favouring the option which has the least environmental risk.
SCENARIO ANALYSIS	An approach to testing the robustness of a policy choice by looking at the effect on the results of assuming different future 'states of the world'.
SCOPING	An initial stage in the appraisal of environmental and other impacts. Possible impacts are listed: the procedure is then to see which impacts need further study and to decide what level of study is needed.
SENSITIVITY ANALYSIS	Analysis of the effects on an appraisal of varying key assumptions and variables.
SSSI	'Site of Special Scientific Interest', an area identified by the Government's advisers on nature conservation as worthy of particular recognition for its flora, fauna or other natural features.
STATISTICAL SIMULATION	A more sophisticated form of sensitivity analysis (qv). The results can be summarised in a variety of statistics.

TRAVEL COST	A valuation technique which uses the expenditure on travel to an environmental resource as a proxy for the value of that resource. See Appendix C, II (ii).
WAGE RISK PREMIA	Pay differentials apparently due to differences in hazards at work.
WEIGHTING AND SCORING	A technique which compares costs and benefits measured in different units by assessing performance against specified criteria, and weighting the results to reflect the relative importance of each criteria.
WILLINGNESS TO PAY and WILLINGNESS TO ACCEPT	Economic concepts which refer to people's expressed preferences to pay for receiving goods or services, or to accept compensation if the goods or services are lost.

Printed in the United Kingdom for HMSO
Dd294618 1/92 C20 G531 10170